# DIVORCE
# AND BEYOND

## Facilitators Manual

## by

## James Greteman, C.S.C.

■

## Leon Haverkamp, M.S.W.

Buckley Publications, Inc.

4848 N. Clark St.
Chicago, Illinois, 60611-4711

**Acknowledgements:**

Carroll, J. Tender of Wishes. (Newman Press, 1969)
Rothluebber, S.S.F., Frences, *Hope, a Meditation*
Satir, V. *Peoplemaking.* (Science Behavior Books, Inc., 1975)

Scripture texts used in this work are taken from the NEW AMERICAN BIBLE, copyright © 1970 by the Confraternity of Christian Doctrine, Washington, D.C. It is used with the permission of the owner, and all rights are reserved.

---

We wish to express our gratitude to the following for their generous contributions to this manual: M. Enright, R. Gross-Berlinger, A.C.S.W., H. Lambin, M.Ed., K. McGowan, A.C.S.W., K. Shannon, M.A., and Rev. Gerard Weber.

---

Library of Congress Catalog No. 82-72048
ISBN No. 915388-17-0
Printed in the United States

---

Edited by: Joseph E. Dunne, Ph.D.
Art and Design: Robert Fairman

# contents

# introduction

You have accepted an invitation to help people by offering them a "safe place" during a critical transition in their lives. We welcome you to a challenging, necessary, and fulfilling experience: ministering to the divorced.

Those of you who are trained psychologists, social workers, group leaders, or counsellors may want to skim through this manual for some specific information for each session. It is for the non-professionals—those of you who have taken on the responsibility of facilitating a group of divorced people for your parish—that this book's detailed explanations are intended. If you're wondering why you ever got into this, what you are going to say, what you are going to do and how you are going to keep everybody from knowing you're scared to death, don't worry. The information and suggestions offered in this manual will help you to become effective and helpful facilitators.

"Divorce and Beyond" is a program developed by Bro. James Greteman, CSC, and Leon Haverkamp, M.S.W., for divorced Catholics. It is intended to help them gain a perspective on their divorce, cope with the stresses and strains associated with divorce, understand some of their emotional responses, and find ways of coping that will lead to growth and the eventual restructuring of their lives. The program consists of eight two-hour meetings plus exercises to be practiced between the sessions. The guide for these sessions is the participant's book for "Divorce and Beyond."

This is a self-help program. It is based upon the premise that sharing one's thoughts, feelings, and experiences with other divorced people is one of the most helpful ways to move beyond the pain of the divorce. You, as the facilitator, have the crucial task of getting the group members to start sharing with each other, and, when necessary, of encouraging them to continue their sharing throughout the program. Your own warmth and caring will provide the momentum and encouragement needed to help your group grow through these sharing sessions.

Ministering to the divorced is not, by any means, the easiest way of expressing your love and concern for others. But we think you will find it, by far, one of the most rewarding ministries. We wish you the best of luck.

## the facilitator's role

- A facilitator is one who "makes things easier, or less difficult; helps forward an action, a process, etc.; assists the progress of a person" (Random House Dictionary).

- Your role in the Divorce and Beyond Program is taking care of all the myriad details that enable a group to function—making the physical arrangements, opening and closing the meetings, keeping the discussions going and on-track, and encouraging the members by being hospitable, listening, and watching. We emphasize again that you are *not* expected to be a leader, a teacher, a counselor, or a healer. It is the members' responsibility to help each other learn and heal. Your responsibility is helping to provide the climate in which this can happen.

- Because the people coming to these groups are in crisis, the sessions deal with highly emotional subjects. Consequently, facilitating these groups calls for a greater sensitivity to emotional overtones than does dealing with most groups.

# ATTITUDES AND SKILLS

- The facilitator should feel comfortable with the subjects being discussed. If you are divorced and have worked through your initial crisis, your experience will give you deeper insights into what is being discussed as well as compassion for the others. However, be careful not to allow any private hangups resulting from your divorce experience to influence the discussions of the group as a whole. If you are not divorced but have strong feelings about it, beware of a natural tendency to be judgmental.

- *CONFIDENTIALITY IS ESSENTIAL.* Remind the group that what is said during the sessions should not be shared with anyone outside the group.

- Respond to your group sincerely, responsibly, and honestly. Avoid the temptation to manipulate the group or any individual, even for a good cause.

- Balance your participation in the discussions: be neither overly active nor quiet to the point of becoming a mystery to the group. Its energies should be devoted to the discussions at hand, not to figuring out "what's with the facilitator."

- Prayer: There are times when group members, or even the group as a whole, are uncomfortable with praying. We feel that prayers are an important part of the healing process, so we have included them throughout the program as suggestions for closing sessions and for members' private use. The prayers offered are all short and directed towards people in crisis. However, if you find that the prayers and meditations suggested are creating more problems than help, by all means feel free to change the closing of the sessions to something more helpful to your group.

# SOME PITFALLS

In dealing with people in pain, it will be impossible for you to be completely objective at all times. Even an experienced and highly motivated facilitator can stumble into certain pitfalls. Here are some common ones to watch out for:

● Caring for people does not mean that you must "fix" them. Avoid falling into the role of "Rescuer." You are not there to solve problems. Your role is to listen attentively and to acknowledge and respect the feelings that are being expressed. The members will help the healing process by themselves when they share their experiences and support each other. This program offers no instant cures or quick solutions.

● Watch your body language. For example, by tightly crossing your arms or turning your shoulders away from the group, you may give the impression that you disapprove of what's being said. By tapping your pencil or having a far-away look in your eyes, you may suggest to the group that you're bored or involved with your own thoughts. In sum, any action that distracts the members or makes them feel unaccepted will make it difficult for them to achieve anything positive. You have to be especially careful about body language during the first couple of meetings, when the participants will be taking their cue from you.

● You will, of course, need to prepare for each session, and, further on in this manual, we will introduce each session and offer suggestions on facilitating each meeting. However, you must resist the temptation to come in with your own game-plan for what *should happen*. The other members may not share your "vision," and you should not attempt to steer them toward a preconceived conclusion.

- Sometimes you may feel troubled by what a group member says. But remember, these sessions deal to a great extent with negative feelings. The members must feel free to express their emotions, and not be inhibited by fears that they will be made to feel foolish, stupid, or bad. Try to convey to the group that all feelings are real and, hence, should be acknowledged and accepted in these sessions. ONE OF THE PURPOSES OF THIS GROUP IS TO HELP THE MEMBERS DEAL WITH THEIR NEGATIVE EMOTIONS IN POSITIVE WAYS.

- Sometimes the group will digress from the discussion questions. As the facilitator, you will have to exercise some judgment and discretion when this occurs. On the one hand, if the digression is into "small talk" that is *totally unrelated* to the purpose of the session, try to bring them back to the topic. If, after you have attempted to bring them back, it becomes apparent that the group is still digressing, it may indicate that they do not feel comfortable with sharing their feelings and opinions on the subject. Or—it may indicate that they are simply bored with the topic. In either case, honor their wishes, and suggest they move on to the next question or exercise.

  On the other hand, if the digression touches on a significant topic that captures the interest of the entire group, it may be desirable to let the digression continue. The questions are primiarly designed as discussion openers, not as rigid schedules. If the group finds better ways to achieve the goal of sharing information, feelings, and insights, all the better. Just be reasonably sure that the group is aware of what is happening, and has freely chosen to pursue this course.

- At the end of each session in the participant's book are suggested activities to further the members' growth. Some members will follow through on these suggestions, but others will not. You will have no control over this beyond encouraging all of them to take some action, however small, and reinforcing those who do so.

- If the session has been particularly emotional, try bringing the group down slowly at least five minutes before you begin the closing part of the session. One good way of diffusing emotion is to insert a question, a general, neutral comment, or even something humorous for them to talk about.

- Sometimes a member may need more help than a self-help group can provide. This will usually become apparent early in the sessions. Your best course of action is to offer alternative sources of help available from local agencies and counselors. Before the sessions begin, check with your parish, your community or diocesan offices for the divorced and separated, Alcoholics Anonymous, Al-Anon, and any other resources that might be available. Then draw up a list of these resources and let the group know at the first session that you have it available.

- DON'T GET UPTIGHT! Experience has proven that these groups are usually made up of caring people. This means that they care about the facilitator as well as about each other. They will be as accepting of your mistakes as they are of their own. They will recognize that you would not have taken on the role of facilitator unless you were a caring person. So long as your warmth and concern come through, don't worry about minor mistakes.

# SPECIAL SITUATIONS

***The Changing Role of the Facilitator:*** The facilitator's role will change during the course of a program. In the beginning, you will do most of the talking in order to get the group started, familiarize the members with the purposes of the program, establish the ground rules, and keep things going till the end of the session. As the members become more familiar with the procedures and more comfortable with each other, they will naturally assume more responsibility during the sessions. This will make it easier for you to participate more in the discussions, if you wish to do so. However, bear in mind that very few groups could ever look upon the facilitator as merely "one of the group." Hence, before "joining in," be sure the group understands that, when you contribute to the discussions, you are *not* speaking as an expert.

Turning the situation around, should the group fail to assume responsiblity in any area, you'll need to do so. For example, the role of timekeeper will probably be yours throughout the sessions.

***The Shy Member:*** In many groups, particularly those dealing with crises, there are members who do not contribute much to the discussions. They may be natural "listeners" rather than "talkers," or they may be afraid to express their opinions or feelings. In either case, make sure they know they are invited to participate but will not be presssured to do so. They will share what they choose to share once they become comfortable with the group. Respect that.

***The Dominating Member:*** During the initial sessions, you will usually find one member who will try to assume control of the meeting. Such a "take-over" person tends to make the other members uneasy, and they will look to you to keep control. Be diplomatic, but make it clear that a self-help group has no leaders. The goal of this group is to learn *from* and *with* other divorced people, as *equals.*

If this person is particularly forceful, and you find yourself unable to cut him/her off diplomatically during the meeting, arrange to meet after the session and explain privately how his/her forceful manner could inhibit the participation of other members of the group.

***The Problem Solver:*** Self-help groups often include an "expert." This person presents a solution as the only alternative and has a way of relating experiences and responding to opposing views that makes the other members feel he or she might have all the answers. The "expert" should be handled in the same way as the dominating member.

***The Emotionally Overwrought Member:*** On occasion, one or more members may want to lead the group into a highly-charged emotional discussion that is unrelated to the session's objectives. If this is allowed to continue, someone may become distraught, or even lose control. Since this is not an Encounter Group, (or unless you are a trained psychologist competent to handle such situations) it will be necessary for you to discreetly calm things down and gently bring the meeting back into focus.

Frequently, when emotional outbursts occur, another member will be alert enough to change the subject, or at least move to a less emotionally-charged plateau, and in so doing, defuse the situation.

It is important, however, that you make it a point to talk to the disturbed member(s) before they leave the meeting. If you feel they need to discuss their emotions or problems in greater depth than can be provided by the support group, put them in contact with someone qualified to help. Your list of professionals will come in handy here (See page 7).

***The Digressor:*** Every group seems to have at least one digressor. We are not referring here to the occasions when the entire *group* decides to digress from the scheduled discussion. We're talking about the *individual* who occasionally strays far afield from the topic and rambles on and on and on. Often, the other group members will handle this themselves. If they do not, it will be up to you, in justice to the whole group, to gently but firmly bring the discussion back to the issue.

***Co-Facilitator:*** If you find the group you are to facilitate is large enough to require breaking down into three or more sub-groups, you might consider bringing in a co-facilitator to help with the exercise discussion. (Some facilitators work as teams. One facilitator assumes the major responsibility for all the sessions—e.g. initial contacts, opening and closing meetings, timekeeping, etc. The co-facilitator helps with the discussions. When the Program is run again with a different group, the roles are reversed.)

If this is a possibility in your area, we encourage you to try it. Besides the obvious advantages to the group, sharing responsibility and having support and a back-up will greatly reduce your susceptibility to "burn-out".

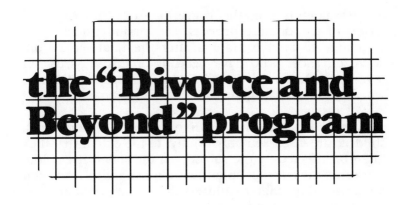

# the "Divorce and Beyond" program

## WHO

*"Divorce and Beyond" has been designed for people who are divorced or who have filed for divorce.* It is not intended for those who are still "on the fence." In the first place, those who have not made a final decision to separate need a different kind of program. Secondly, there is a remote chance that the group could be sued if it were found to be instrumental in encouraging someone to divorce.

*Note:* Be sure this distinction is made clear in your publicity and organizing procedures, though you need not require a legal document. Furthermore, when you first contact a potential group member, you should reiterate that the program is only for those who have at least begun legal proceedings for a divorce.

To help yourself relate to the people who come to support groups, keep in mind that they are not psychologically ill; they are just looking for some help during this crisis. This program focuses on the difficulties and emotions that

are prevalent during the transition—or "mourning"—
period of the divorce process. this period usually lasts
from nine to twelve months after the final separation.
However, those who have been divorced for years but
have not effectively dealt with this stage would also
benefit from this program.

The sessions deal with the divorced people themselves.
Children are discussed only briefly, to the extent that they
might be affected by the subject matter under discussion.
Too often divorced people focus almost entirely on their
children and thus fail to address their own problems. The
goal here is to help divorced people, including those who
are parents, reach some understanding and stability in
their lives. When they achieve this, they will be better able
to understand the problems of their children and to offer
them some stability.

## WHAT

*A Self-Help Group:* This, of course, indicates that there
are no leaders, teachers, counselors, or healers. The main
responsibility for what happens rests with the group itself.
Some *information* is provided in the brief readings ac-
companying each session. However, the primary source of
*learning* is through the sharing of experiences, feelings,
and insights with other divorced people during the discussions. The *growth* will come from what each member
chooses to do with what he or she has learned.

*A Closed Group:* People coming to these sessions are
looking for more support than "rap" groups can give.
They are asked to devote time and effort to working
through the problems and emotions that emerge during
the early stage of their divorce, and to share deep feelings
and sensitive experiences with each other. But the members will not feel free to experience strong emotions and

share their feelings until they become comfortable and learn to trust each other. A closed group can provide the stability and the atmosphere that foster ease and trust. (Because this closeness is necessary for the group to succeed, we strongly recommend that new people who wish to join after a group has started be asked to wait until a new group can be formed.) In this way they too, will benefit fully from the program.

## SIZE OF GROUP

These groups work best with a minimum of six and a maximum of fifteen participants. If more than fifteen people are available for a group, consider starting a second group at another time or with another facilitator.

## STRUCTURE OF PROGRAM

The members are asked to commit themselves to eight two-hour sessions. One of your most important tasks will be to act as a timekeeper, to see to it that the sessions start and end on time. Holding to the schedule is important for two reasons. First, you are keeping your side of the agreement. Second, the members are more likely to be prompt and to stick to the business at hand when they know the time is strictly limited.

The general format for each session is:

A) OPENING: Group members share with each other what they have done during the week with the suggested exercises. The sharing is totally optional, but you will usually find that those who have done something will want to talk about it. Their example, in turn, will encourage the others to practice the exercises during the following week.

B) READING: The readings are intentionally brief. After all, entire volumes have been written on each subject. Their purpose is to give you some content upon which to base the discussions.

C) DISCUSSION: The discussion questions and exercises are not meant to be quizzes; they are simply suggestions for starting the discussions and keeping them focused on the issues. How they are used within the program is entirely up to you and the group. (You will find more extensive hints on handling the discussions on pages 19 and 20 in this manual.

D) CLOSING: Sum up the discusssion or share ideas from other sub-groups (if you have any), then close session.

E) DURING THE WEEK: The program carries on the process between sessions by offering suggestions to help them improve their self-esteem, deal with stress, reflect more deeply on how the week's topic affects their lives, and offers brief prayers. Some activities are one-time only exercises; others are meant to be practiced until they become habitual. The participants are certainly not expected to do all the suggested exercises during the week, but we do urge each member to CHOOSE AT LEAST ONE EXERCISE EACH WEEK.

## WHEN

We suggest that the sessions be held one week apart. This interval maintains the flow of the process, and still allows the members time to practice their daily exercises. If this is not feasible, meeting every other week can be a workable alternative. When offering the program to your community, take into consideration the special restrictions put on people's schedules during the summer and Christmas time.

## WHERE

This is up to you and your group sponsor. If the church or rectory has a comfortable room, by all means use it! Church and school facilities are neutral territory for everyone. If you must use a private home, take steps to insure the privacy of the group. Make some arrangements so that the person whose home you use doesn't spend too much time playing host or hostess, and, if necessary, find someone outside the group to answer the telephone and the door so that the group will be disrupted as little as possible.

## WHY

Divorced Catholics have needed a program of this sort for a long time. They need to work through the "mourning" period with others who know, understand, and share their special problems and frustrations. They need this "safe-place" to meet other divorced Catholics who are working toward the same goals.

Why are you, the facilitator, involved in this program? We can only surmise that you recognize the problems divorced people face today, and have enough courage and loving concern to attempt this challenging ministry.

# NOTES

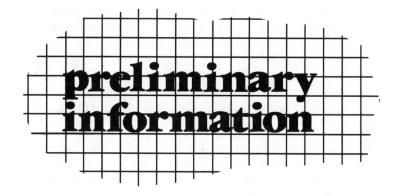

# preliminary information

1. In your announcements, make it clear that this program is for people who are already divorced or who have at least filed for divorce.

2. Interview people before accepting them into the group. Inform them of the scope of this program. (See pages 12–15). If a personal interview is impractical, at least talk to each prospective member over the telephone.

3. Decide if you are going to give each member a copy of the Participants' book gratis, or charge for it. Be sure each potential member is aware at the first contact/interview of any charges or fees deemed necessary.

4. Obtain the following information and keep it handy during the sessions: name, address, home telephone number, work telephone number, the number of children and their ages, how long married, how long divorced. In the beginning sessions, this information will help you to identify group members and address personal, relevant comments to them.

5. Once the group has started, do not allow others to attend the meetings. The presence of observers tends to make the members feel threatened and to inhibit the free flow of the discussions. It would be of great value if a parish priest or minister would attend the first session to welcome the group. However, after the first session, only facilitator(s) and members should be present.

6. Although you cannot control what anyone in your group does outside the meetings, you should suggest to them that socializing after the sessions (dating, going to bars, etc.) will only work against a sense of community and group support. If they wish to socialize on this level, they should do so at times other than meeting nights.

7. Permit no alcoholic beverages at the sessions. However, coffee is often helpful after the sessions when some members wish to stay and keep the discussions going.

8. Start and end each meeting within 15 minutes of the scheduled time. Some members may have other appointments or be restricted by the needs of babysitters, transportation, etc. Those who wish to continue the discussions can do so after the session has formally closed—provided that the room is available and you have the time.

# suggestions for exercises

***(Applicable to all Sessions)***

1. If there are more than eight members in your group, break them up into sub-groups of no more than six people. You may get some resistance to this. For example, the talkers in your groups will want everyone to hear what they have to say. But those members who are not so assertive will feel freer to talk in a smaller group and will have more opportunities to do so. Should they be left only in a large group where they feel "shut out," they might well drop out of the program.

2. If you break your group into sub-groups, make sure each of them has some writing surface.

3. If possible, place yourself where you can be aware of what is taking place in each sub-group. You want to avoid continually moving from group to group and thereby disrupting the discussions.

4. Keep the members in the same sub-groups for the full session. However, group members may form new sub-groups for each subsequent meeting if they prefer.

5. Two exercises are provided for each session. Usually, the first exercise contains the most important material. The time allotted for both exercises is an hour and a half, but if the group decides to keep discussing one exercise (or one question) for the entire time, allow this to happen. Just make sure that the discussions are relevant (and not continual repetitions of opposing views), and that all of the members are fully aware of this decision.

6. For the remaining exercises or questions, the members can decide at the end of the session whether they would prefer to (a) complete the exercises at home during the week, (b) add another session to their commitment and complete this material at the following meeting, or (c) skip it entirely.

7. The exercises and questions are provided only to foster discussion and to focus some attention on the problems that are covered in the readings. They are not quiz or examination questions. Hence, they are to be used during the meetings only to the extent that they foster sharing and learning among the members.

8. Call for a halt and a stretch, if you feel it is warranted, after about 45 minutes of discussion. However, when the discussions are really going well, try to maintain the continuity by postponing the break or, at least, by keeping it short (a "five-minute break" will almost always turn into a fifteen-minute one).

9. Discussion/exercises should be limited to between 1¼–1½ hours to allow time for opening and closing meetings.

# session ONE

## The Process of Divorce

As in most programs, the people who come to this first meeting will be unfamiliar with the program and unacquainted with you and with one another. They won't know what to expect or what is expected of them. Some may find it difficult to talk in a group under any circumstances. Others may find it difficult to talk about something so personal and so emotionally charged as their divorce. Still others may find it hard to wind down once they've started.

To help you over this first hurdle, we are providing you with a great deal of information to use as a checklist.

*Space and materials:* You will need a comfortable room that affords privacy, good lighting, and a comfortable amount of space so that the group feels neither hemmed-in nor dwarfed. You will need pencils, name tags, a marking pen (if the name tags are not prepared before the meeting), a writing surface (a table, a writing board, a sheet of cardboard) for each member, and a copy of the participant's book for each member. If refreshments are to be served after the session, provide one or more beverages (coffee, tea, or soft drinks), cups, glasses, sugar, cream, and snacks.

*Welcome* each member individually as he or she arrives. If possible, have the name tags prepared (first names will do). Be sure to start the meeting no later than 15 minutes after the scheduled time, to get the group into the habit of starting on time.

*Opening:* Have the people sit in a circle or around a table.

1. Ask the members to introduce themselves to the others by saying their first name and telling how long they were married, how long they have been separated and/or divorced, the number of children, if any, and briefly, what they expect from this program. Start off with yourself.

2. Introduce the program by explaining the following in your own words:

   (a) This is a program for divorced people who are psychologically healthy, but who are working through the hurts, frustrations, and mixed-up emotions that accompany most crises. (If any member feels that they need more help than a self-help group can provide, advise them that you have a list of professional people and agencies who are better qualified to meet their needs.)

   (b) It is for those who want to learn something and grow from this painful experience so that they can begin rebuilding a happier, fulfilled life as a single.

   (c) This program requires some work as well as listening and talking.

   (d) This program is designed for closed groups and requires a commitment to at least four of the eight two-hour sessions. It takes time and a consistent group for people to develop a sense of belonging and to grow comfortable with each other. The meetings are scheduled one (or two) weeks apart.

(e)  Format of meetings: An opening, a reading, two exercises, and a closing. (Note: A very important part of the program takes place between the sessions, when members are urged to do the "During the Week" exercises. Talking with the others is of great importance, but the members will greatly enhance the healing process by doing something with what they have learned.)

***The Reading*** (5 minutes): The reading for this session begins on page 9. The readings will be more effective if they are read aloud by different people, each taking no more than two paragraphs. Ask for a volunteer to start. Suggest that the group pay particular attention to the section dealing with the Mourning Period, since this is the focus of the entire program.

***Break into small groups,*** if necessary. Usually, the time allotted for the discussions is from 1¼ to 1½ hours. However, there will be less time for the discussions at this first session because of the greater amount of time required for the Opening. Note the time when you break for the exercises, allow another 15 minutes for the Closing, then advise the group how much time they have left to work on the two exercises.

***Exercise One*** focuses on their feelings when they first realized that their marriage relationship was over, and how those feelings have changed since then. It attempts to get the members to vocalize the many negative emotions they may be feeling so that, with the group's help, they can deal with them more constructively.

***Exercise Two*** focuses on the "real world" problems that face the divorced while they are trying to work through their emotions.

*Five-Minute Warning:* Advise the members when they have five minutes left so that they can wind up their discussions.

*Closing* (15–20 minutes): If you have divided the members into sub-groups, bring them back together.

- Since the main purpose of this program is to foster understanding and acceptance through sharing, there is no need to summarize or analyze the ideas covered in each session. However, inquire if there is anything that one sub-group wishes to share with the others.

- Point out that there are pages after each session for them to jot down what they wish to remember from the session.

- Repeat your opening reminder that the value of the program depends to a great extent on what they do with what they have learned. For this session, only one Reflection exercise is offered for "During the Week," but it is a very important one. Writing out their "story" and adding to it or deleting from it as their perceptions change is a valuable tool in understanding and accepting their own history.

- If the members have not already done so, set the date, time, and place for the next meeting. If they have done this earlier, remind them.

- Ask if anyone has difficulties with transportation, babysitting, or other logistic matters. Perhaps others in the group could be of assistance. Suggest they exchange information after the meeting is closed.

- Close each session with something short, meaningful to the group, and comfortable for you. We suggest a relaxing exercise, a short prayer, or both. Because of the length of this first session and your promise to conclude the session reasonably close to the scheduled time, we would suggest you close this session with the following short prayer:

## Serenity Prayer

God, give us grace to accept with serenity the things that cannot be changed, courage to change the things which should be changed, and the wisdom to distinguish the one from the others.

(Reinhold Niebuhr)

# NOTES

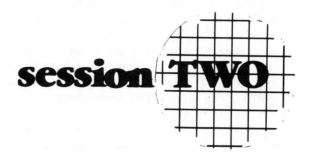

# session TWO

## Self-Image

*Introduction:* Professionals who deal with divorcing people tell us that about 90% of them have suffered some damage to their self-esteem. This holds true no matter who initiated the divorce. The intensity of the damage varies with their feelings of failure and rejection. Until they begin to feel better about themselves, until they can see themselves as complete, competent, lovable, and loving persons, they will have a hard time working out of this divorce crisis.

*Materials:* Same as for Session One, except that you can eliminate the name tags if you feel that they are no longer needed.

*Opening* (15–20 minutes): Open the meeting on time and make any necessary announcements. Ask if anyone has anything to offer the group from the experience of writing his or her "story" during the past week. Encourage those who have started. Do not, however, make those who neglected to do it feel that they have flunked their homework. Reinforce the idea that these daily exercises between sessions are not "busy-work" but a way of getting through the mourning period a little more easily and swiftly.

Sometimes a member will want to discuss a question or problem that came up during the preceding week but may feel reluctant to do so during the session if the matter is not related to the assigned topics. Inquire now whether anyone feels the need to raise a question, but WATCH THE TIME. If someone becomes long-winded at this time, gently close them off by suggesting that, in justice to those who must leave on schedule, further discussion of this matter be postponed until after the meeting. Those who can remain after the session can continue the discussion over coffee, if your time and the facilities permit.

*Reading* (5 minutes): Refer to page 21 in the participant's book. This reading is very short because the exercises take up a great deal of time. Ask that each member read one paragraph aloud, and ask for a volunteer to start.

*Break into sub-groups,* if necessary. Set the time when the discussions should end. The combined time for both exercises should be about 1½ hours, but be sure to allow enough time for closing off the meeting.

*Exercise One:* Professionals emphasize low self-esteem in their profiles of divorced people. However, it is still up to the individual members to evaluate how they feel about themselves. This exercise directs them to reflect on how they felt about themselves at the time of their divorce and on some of the good things that they feel about themselves now.

*Exercise Two:* This attempts to help the members evaluate their self-image through the use of a chart listing personal characteristics, followed by reflective questions about (1) how they feel their self-image affects the way they relate to others, and (2) how they can improve their self-image.

A valuable corollary to this exercise is to attempt to discover if the image they have of themselves is the same image they project to others. But, because of their vulnerability at this time, we have added the second graph (How Do You See Me?) as an optional exercise to do privately with someone they respect and trust.

*Five-Minute Warning:* Advise the members when they have five minutes left to wind up their discussions.

*Closing* (15–20 minutes):

- If you divided the members into sub-groups for the discussion, bring them together again for the remainder of the session.

- Ask whether anyone would like to share anything from their discussions with those who were not in their group.

- Point out that on page 29 there is an optional exercise (How Do You See Me) for those who would like to work this exercise out with someone else in order to see what image they project to others.

- Emphasize that, from now on, more than one suggestion will be offered for the exercises to be done during the week. Although they are not expected to do all the exercises, they are to choose at least one. Some suggestions will be "one-time only" exercises, designed to elicit insights or to develop self-esteem. Other exercises are designed to be practiced daily until they become a habit. If any member chooses the habit-forming exercises, suggest they keep practicing it for at least a week. If after a week's practice, the suggestion is not helpful to them, they can try the suggestion offered the following week. The more exercises they work to develop better habits, the better they will feel about themselves and others, and the quicker they will work out of this "Mourning Period." However, the "During the Week" exercises should be presented in such a way as to offer them hope of improving, not to add another pressure to their lives.

- Remind group of date, time, and place of next meeting.
- Close the meeting (see the suggestion below).
- "Coffee and."

## SUGGESTION FOR CLOSING
### (2 minutes)

We have suggested for this week's "During the Week" self-affirmation exercise that they use the "pot" image. The following relaxation exercise is a good lead-in.

Ask the group to sit quietly for a few minutes, and:

1. Close their eyes
2. Take a deep breath
3. Hold it for several seconds
4. Slowly let it out
5. Repeat this breathing exercise three times

When the group is relaxed, try reading the following *slowly* (you may want to practice it a few times before the first meeting):

Imagine that you are a large pot. Whatever is in your pot is what you must live with and what you have to share with others. (Wait 10 seconds.) Some of the things in your pot you have shared with us this evening. Reflect back on some of these things. (Wait 10 seconds.) However, you can control what goes into your pot. You *can* keep your pot filled with things that make you feel good. You *can* share that goodness with others. (Wait 10 seconds.)

(Adapted from Virginia Satir's *Peoplemaking.)*

Conclude with the following short prayer:

O Lord, only You are perfect. And You don't expect perfection from me. But I am trying to be a little better today than I was yesterday. Growing and changing are not easy, Lord. Please help me!

## DURING THE WEEK

*Reflection:* Continue the "story" notebook exercise by having them write how they felt about themselves during the various periods of their lives.

*Stress:* Some exercises for stress and self-affirmation can be done at the same time, since their purposes are similar. One of the most effective anti-stress helps is to set aside some "free" time. This is quiet time to be alone, calm down, and enjoy a little breathing space.

*Self-Affirmation:* Suggest that they devote some of the "free" time mentioned above to continue with the meditation that was used to close this week's session, by putting some positives into their pot. (Suggestions for some "positives" are included in the participant's book, page 27.)

# NOTES

# session THREE

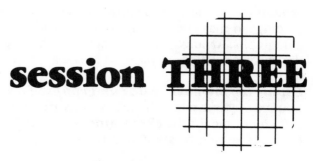

## Stress

**Introduction:** This session points out how much stress divorced people are subjected to and how it affects their energy levels and their health. There is positive stress as well as negative stress, but too much of either kind can make people ill. As the members become more aware of these effects, they will, hopefully, resolve to reduce their stress to a manageable level so that they will have the energy to handle their other problems.

**Materials:** Same as for Session Two.

**Opening** (15–20 minutes): Open the meeting on time (just knowing that something in their lives will be on schedule should relieve some of their stress.) Make any necessary announcements. Ask if anyone would like to tell the group something about his or her "During the Week Exercise." If there is still time after this, ask whether anyone would like to comment on something that happened during the week. (Again, watch the time, and gently set limits on anyone in your group who seems like a constant "dumper.")

**Reading** (5 minutes): Refer to page 35 in participant's book. Ask for a volunteer to start reading aloud. Go around the circle and have other members continue the reading, so that one person does not read more than two paragraphs. Arrange for a member of each sub-group to do the second reading on page 38 at the appropriate time.

*Divide the members into sub-groups,* if necessary. Announce the time when the discussions are to end, allowing sufficient time for the closing (the combined time for both exercises should be about 1½ hours).

*Exercise One:* Deals with worry, anxiety, and the "flooding of emotions"—all of which contribute greatly to stress. The discussion, however, centers on the *causes* of the fears and anxieties, both at the time of the divorce and now.

*Exercise Two:* Deals with the problem of overload. It asks the members to evaluate the stress level in their lives by working the "Life Change Index Scale," and gives some clues as to why some people are affected more than others by the same amount of stress. The questions ask the members how stress affects them physically and how they cope with it.

*Five-Minute Warning:* Advise the members when only five minutes remain for the discussions, so they have time for a wind-up.

*Closing* (15–20 minutes): If there are sub-groups, bring them back together.

- Ask whether there is anything that one group wishes to share with the others.

- Point out that some suggestions for relieving stress by changing attitudes are provided at the end of this week's "During the Week" exercises (see page 44).

Urge the group to read these suggestions during the week.

- Reemphasize the need to do at least one of the suggested exercises during the coming week.

- Close the meeting (see the suggestion below).

- "Coffee and."

## SUGGESTION FOR CLOSING
### (2 minutes)

Try another exercise in using imagery to relax. This is a lead-in to the "garden" image contained in the self-affirmation exercise suggested for the coming week. Those who did not respond to the "pot" image may respond to this one. Start with the breathing exercise, as you did last week (see page 30). When the group has relaxed, read the following *slowly:*

> Imagine that your mind is a garden. What you sow in that garden is what you will reap. (Wait 10 seconds.) You can continue allowing the seeds of self-doubt and fear to grow, or you can begin planting seeds of hope, peace, and joy. (Wait 10 seconds.) What weeds do you want to pull from your garden now? What special seeds do you want to plant? (Wait 10 seconds.)

*Concluding prayer:*

> O Lord, You invited those of us who are weary and burdened to come to You and be refreshed. So here I am, Lord, in need of Your support and trusting in Your love.

# DURING THE WEEK

*Reflection:* This adds another dimension to their "story." A strong *faith* in God, and *hope* that accompanies such faith, often enables people to cope with a great deal of stress. This week's suggestion is to see how the faith of the members has been affected by their divorce. This reflection asks about their feelings toward God, the Church, and religion.

*Self-Affirmation:* Continue the use of imagery to reinforce the "positives" in their lives. Using the same imagery as your closing (the garden,) gives some additional positive thoughts to plant in the subconscious.

*Stress:* Getting rid of some of the "load" of duties and concerns is a major requirement for managing stress. This week's suggestion offers ways of handling some of the tasks they feel they must complete this week.

*SPECIAL NOTE FOR YOU:* The group members are not the only ones under stress. Be careful of the stress in your own life or you may soon "burn out." Make it a point to do something special to relax after each session. Find someone competent and trustworthy you can talk to—another facilitator, your priest or minister, someone from another divorce group, a counselor—anyone with whom you can share some of your feelings about the group and whom you can count on to answer some of your questions. You need support both to maintain your own equilibrium and to continue giving so much of yourself as a facilitator.

# session FOUR

## Anger

*Introduction:* Because of the great impact that anger has on the lives and relationships of divorced people—indeed, on everyone—the next two sessions are devoted to it:

SESSION FOUR:  Focuses on what anger is, and where and how we learned to respond to it.

SESSION FIVE:  Focuses on the different ways people express their anger, and how these expressions affect them and others.

Although this material is broken down into three readings and four exercises, the various aspects of anger are obviously interrelated. If possible, however, hold off the discussion on how the members express their anger until the fifth session. (Note: Occasionally a group will be able to work through all this material in one session. If this happens in your group, choose an exercise from a previous session or do one of the Alternate Sessions in lieu of Session Five.)

*Material:* Same as in the previous session.

*Opening* (15–20 minutes): Open the meeting on time. Make any necessary announcements. Inquire if anyone would like to comment on their "During the Week" exercises or on something that happened during the week.

*Reading* (5 minutes): Arrange for volunteers to read both parts of the reading, as you did in Session Three. The reading for the whole group is on page 49; the second reading for the sub-groups is on page 51.

*Break into sub-groups,* if necessary. Set a time limit for the discussions.

*Exercise One:* This attempts to help the members identify with whom or at what they are angry. This, at first glance, would seem to belabor the obvious. But experience has shown that many people have difficulties admitting they're angry with someone, particularly when they love, admire, or feel grateful to that person. Similarly, they often have problems seeing how their anger—expressed, suppressed, or repressed—affects their relationships.

*Exercise Two:* Focuses on where the members learned their ways of expressing anger. Once they see the relationship between the patterns they grew up with and their present behavior, they will find it easier to make needed modifications.

*NOTE:* Some people tend to redirect their anger at anyone who doesn't take their side or understand what they've been upset about. This can be very intimidating and destructive within a discussion group. If you see a member begin taking out his or her anger on another member, be sure to intervene quickly, bring the discussion back to the issues, and cool things down.

*Five-Minute Warning:* Advise the members when they have five minutes left for discussion. If you notice that a sub-group's discussions have been particularly hot, insert a comment, a question, or some humor to help those members cool down before they rejoin the others for the closing.

*Closing* (10–15 minutes): If the members have been divided into sub-groups, bring them back together.

- Ask if any sub-group has something from its discussions that it would like to share with the others.

- Stress the necessity for reading the essay in preparation for next week's meeting. This selection is much too long to read during the session, and it requires some reflection by the members to identify some of their own roles.

- Urge them to continue doing at least one exercise during the week.

- Close.

- "Coffee and."

## SUGGESTION FOR CLOSING

By this time, you're probably a pro at leading the relaxation and meditation exercises, so we'll continue with another one on Hope. The following excerpt is the opening of a long meditation by Frances Rothluebber, SSF. We will continue with this meditation as a closing suggestion for the rest of the session.

Start with the breathing exercises (see page 30).

When the group is relaxed, read the following *slowly:*

> Every beginning is a home for hope.
> A seed is a home for hope.

To say YES to the beginning is to say YES to what will become.

To say YES to the dawn is to say YES to the day and the night.

To say YES to the knock is to say YES to the friendship.

Hope speaks: YES!

Imagine a sower going out to sow.

Imagine LIFE moving out over time and across space to sow hope.

Imagine LIFE going out to sow.

And a seed falls into our hands.

A now-seed is in the cup of our hands.

*Concluding prayer:*

We have in our hands, Lord, the now-seed that has been given us to start rebuilding a new life. Give us your strength and your wisdom to help us plant our seed well, so that soon our Hope will be our Reality.

## DURING THE WEEK

*Reflection:* Has them continue with their "story" notebook by adding why, how, and at whom they have expressed their anger during the various stages in their lives. They are to give particular emphasis to their current feelings and expressions of anger.

*Self-Affirmation:* To reinforce their self-affirmation, this exercise uses a visual aid: an outline of a tree with roots and leaves in which they are to write the positive things about themselves that they feel or have heard others say.

*Stress:* The members are asked to keep a simple diary of their eating, sleeping and relaxing patterns. Their successive goals are to (1) learn what their patterns are, (2) modify the patterns in order to achieve a better balance in their lives, and (3) thereby gain more energy to deal with everyday problems.

*Prayer:* This session adds the element of prayer. It suggests three ways of praying: (1) a simple talk with God, (2) centering prayer, and (3) meditation fantasy. Although some members may be unacquainted with the latter two methods, don't hesitate to recommend them as relaxation techniques as well as approaches to prayer. (The "hope" excerpts suggested as closings are forms of centering prayer.)

# NOTES

# session FIVE

## More Anger

*Introduction:* (See Session Four, page 37.)

*Materials:* Same as for the previous sessions.

*Opening* (15–20 minutes): Open the meeting on time. Make any necessary announcements. Ask whether anyone would like to comment on his or her experiences with the "During the Week" exercises or on something that happened during the week.

*Reading:* Ask who has done the reading for this session (pages 59 to 65 in participant's book). If they have all read the material, they can break into sub-groups and begin Exercise One. If three or four have not read the material, suggest that they form a sub-group and read it together before beginning the discussions. The others can start Exercise One immediately. If only one or two people have not done the reading, suggest that they read it quietly by themselves while the others go on to the discussion. If most of your group has failed to read the material, you will have to read it during the session. In this case, ask for volunteers to read each "role" aloud, but *skip reading the suggestions following each role.* This will save some time here; the members can come back to the suggestions that apply to them during the exercise.

**Break into sub-groups,** if necessary. Set a time for the discussions to end, allowing enough time for the closing (the combined time for the reading and both exercises should be about 1 ¾ hours).

**Exercise One:** Ask the members to identify which anger roles apply to them, and to share what happens when they express their anger toward people who are important to them.

**Exercise Two:** Ask the members to look at the anger "roles" played by people who are close to them, and to think of more constructive ways of handling their anger with these people.

**Five-Minute Warning:** Advise the members when they have five minutes to wind up their discussions.

**Closing** (10–15 minutes): If the members have been divided into sub-groups, bring them back together.

- Ask whether any sub-group wants to comment on something from its discussions.

- Point out that some hints on how to change one's behavior are offered on page 70.

- Make a strong pitch for working daily on at least one of the suggestions in the "During the Week" exercises.

- Close the meeting.
- "Coffee and."

## SUGGESTION FOR CLOSING

Continue with the Hope meditation. Start with the breathing exercises on page 30. When the group has relaxed, read the following *slowly:*

Every beginning is a home for hope.

A seed is a home for hope.

Can a hundred yesterdays eat up all energy, consume all hope?

Who decides when the seed is dying?

Or who decides that the seed lives and must be replanted?

We can hold the seed, refusing to believe new beginnings are necessary, saying: "Surely, today will have a tomorrow."

We can clutch the seed fearfully, knowing that a seed released can whirl to its death in a progress wind, knowing that the birds of change could peck it to death.

We can grasp it, cradling it, fearing that the sun of new thought may be too strong.

We can say, "This is a tired seed, life has gone from it.

Is it really needed?

Is the fruit already stale in the seed?"

*Concluding prayer:*

> When we've been hurt, it's hard for us to trust,
>     O Lord.
> When we're fearful, it's hard for us to believe in
>     a better tomorrow.
> Only faith makes this possible.
> We ask You to strengthen our faith so that we
>     may hope.

## DURING THE WEEK

*Reflection:* This has them continue their "story note-books" by reflecting on how they expressed their anger during the different chapters of their lives, and by noticing how their anger patterns may have changed over the years. It asks them to write down why they respond to anger the way they do now, and suggests that they practice one of the ways offered in the reading for handling their anger more constructively.

*Self-Affirmation:* This is another role-playing exercise. It attempts to reinforce the "positives" in their lives by asking them to look at themselves from the viewpoint of someone who really likes and approves of them.

*Stress:* This is one exercise that most people will have very little difficulty practicing. It calls for recreation, some fun, and the putting aside of problems for a short while every day.

# session SIX

## Blame and Guilt

*Introduction:* Blame and guilt play major roles in the lives of divorced people, particularly the newly divorced. Because these feelings are so closely allied, we have put them together in one session. Since most divorced people are deeply into blaming, the exercise on this subject is placed first. Guilt also needs to be explored. However, inasmuch as it seldom elicits the same degree of free expression, the discussions on it tend to be more constrained.

*Materials:* Same as for the previous sessions.

*Opening* (15–20 minutes): Open the meeting on time. Make any necessary announcements. Inquire about group's experiences during the week (both with the exercises and in their lives). Again, encourage the members to keep practicing at least one exercise every day if they want to see results.

*Reading* (5 minutes): Arrange for volunteers to read aloud the preliminary readings, as you did in the previous sessions. The first reading (for the whole group) is on page 75; the second reading (in sub-groups) in on page 78.

***Break into sub-groups,*** if necessary. Announce the time when the discussions are to end.

***Exercise One:*** This exercise asks the members to identify whomever they blame for the breakup of their marriage, and to consider how their blaming attitude affects their relationships with these people. It also attempts to provide some insights into how the members feel when they are being blamed. Talking about blame usually opens floodgates of emotions from the group—particularly of anger. A great deal of time can be spent on rehashing Sessions Four and Five. Try to keep this to a minimum. If the group chooses to spend the entire 1½ hours discussing blame, make sure that all the members are aware that this would postpone or eliminate their discussion of guilt, and that they all agree to this.

***Exercise Two:*** As we mentioned in the Introduction, groups often have mixed feelings when discussing guilt. Divorced people often feel guilty without knowing why. Furthermore, given their present circumstances, they are often unsure of what to do about it. Some may be struggling with the meaning of adult conscience and moral responsibilities, and they may not be fully aware of the emphasis on healing in the new approaches to reconciliation.

This exercise is not intended to be an open confession—God forbid! The reading focuses on the members' feelings of guilt stemming from their divorce and attempts to put these feelings into some kind of perspective. Its ultimate purpose is helping the members discard some of the bags of imposed guilt that they may have been carrying around for years.

***Five-Minute Warning:*** Notify the members when they have five minutes left to wind up their discussions.

*Closing* (10–15 minutes): If the members have been divided into sub-groups, bring them back together.

- Ask if anyone wants to share something with the other sub-groups.

- If any of the groups did not get around to Exercise Two, urge them to do this at home as their "During the Week" exercise. Better yet, suggest that this exercise is important enough to warrant an added session.

- If your group did discuss guilt, chances are that the discussions became quite heavy and that the members are feeling rather low. Do what you can to lighten things up a bit before you close the session. (You might also consider following this up at some future time by planning a liturgy or inviting a priest or minister to talk to the group.) In any event, emphasize that a loving God offers forgiveness to everyone.

- Mention again the importance of continuing the exercises during the week.

- One of the optional sessions offered is on Forgiveness (see page 105 in participants' book).

  Suggest to your group that this topic is particularly appropriate after working through guilt and blame. Ask their opinion about adding a session to work through this material. (It could be inserted before or after the session on Loneliness.)

  If the group decides against adding another meeting to their original commitment, suggest they read this essay during the coming week, work on the exercises by themselves, and perhaps do some meditation on the subject.

- Close the meeting.

- "Coffee and."

## SUGGESTION FOR CLOSING

Continue with the meditation on Hope. Start with the breathing exercises (see page 30). When the group has relaxed, read the following *slowly:*

Every beginning is a home for hope.

A seed is a home for hope.

The soil is different now. There is a raw new texture to the quality.

The earth, sand, and rocks are shifting, convulsing.

Can this seed grow?

Already in the heart of this seed, hope struggles, stirs.

Every new moment has potential,
A possible awakening,
A fresh surge to meet difficulties.

Already new questions, new desires, new dreams move.

We are renewed by crisis, summoned to rebirth.

Hope is in the struggle itself.

Hope grows in darkness;
Night is a time for growth.

Hope watches through the night to know the dawn-moment
To blossom in welcome.

Because of God-Present
We have FAITH to HOPE.

The future grows secretly, quietly, irresistibly.

The light stored in the soil awakens the future.

From small, hopeless, unlikely beginnings . . .
unimaginable endings.

**Concluding Prayer** *(Paraphrase of Psalm 19):*

I have a course which I must travel.
It is not easy; I make so many mistakes.
I am plagued with faults and obsessions.
O God, forbid that these should destroy me.
Set me free from their tenacious hold on me.
Encompass me with Your love and grace
    that these things may not stand
    between You and me.

Amen

## DURING THE WEEK

*Reflection:* In continuing their story and reflecting on the values that guided their past choices, the members will come to see which of their values seem absolute and which have changed over the years. The emphasis, however, is on the present. They are asked to list the values that guide them now as they choose their present and future courses of action.

*Self-Affirmation:* An easy exercise. It suggests that the members do something special this week to recognize, and reward themselves for all the things they have accomplished.

*Stress:* This exercise explains to the members the procedures that you followed in closing the second and third sessions (the "pot" and the "garden" images), and suggests they try doing some guided imagery for themselves.

# NOTES

# session SEVEN

## Loneliness

***Introduction:*** This session attempts to make the distinction between being *lonely* (both socially and emotionally) and being *alone.* The readings emphasize that loneliness is a problem for all human beings—single or married. Particular attention is given to the special lonely feelings of the newly divorced and the ways they often react to their loneliness. Finally, the session aims at helping the members see that, even in a couple-centered world, being a single and alone does not mean being an incomplete person.

***Material:*** Same as for the previous sessions.

***Reading*** (5 minutes): As you did in the previous sessions. First reading (entire group), page 85; second reading (sub-groups), page 88.

***Break into sub-groups,*** if necessary. Set the time when the discussions are to end.

***Exercise One:*** This focuses on the social isolation that abruptly hits many people when they divorce. The discussion questions deal with their present feelings of loneliness (the loneliness they felt during their marriage is taken up in the Reflection exercise for During the Week).

Many groups will naturally turn to the subject of dating (whom to date, where to find dates, the challenges and frustrations of relearning the dating game). If this happens in your group, draw the members' attention to the "Word of Caution" at the end of the reading about loneliness, warning divorced people about forming serious relationships too soon. Note: The discussions for this session will tend to be more subdued than those at other sessions. The members' ability to share their lonely feelings with the group will depend on a great many factors—how long they were married, how long they have been divorced, who has custody of the children, how active they are, how assertive they are, etc. Furthermore, lonely feelings that are less intense and lack particular associations are very hard to talk about.

***Exercise Two:*** This exercise focuses on emotional loneliness and its usual counterpart—feeling incomplete because one is single. It is often hard for groups to distinguish between social loneliness and what this program calls "emotional loneliness." Being without someone with whom one has shared a good part of one's life is certainly an emotional experience! The distinction made here is that people often feel lonely even when they are in groups or are living with a mate. Others can be physically alone but not feel lonely at all. The exercise makes the point that divorced people are complete persons, and that their emotional survival does not depend on their being part of a couple.

***Five-Minute Warning:*** Advise the members when they have five minutes to wind up their discussions.

*Closing* (15–20 minutes): Bring the members together again if they have been divided into sub-groups.

- Ask whether anyone wishes to share anything with the other sub-groups.

- Urge the members to keep working on the "During the Week" exercises.

- Remind the group of the date, time, and place of next meeting.

- Mention to the group that time management is one way of dealing with loneliness. Point out that some methods are offered on page 92 and suggest that they take some of their leisure time this week to read this material.

- Unless the group has decided to hold additional sessions, next week's will be the wind-up session. To close the program, it is a good idea to plan a special celebration (e.g., a closing ceremony, a party, a liturgy). Ask for ideas, call for a decision, and ask for volunteers to help with the arrangements. (On page 61 are three suggestions for closing the final session short enough to allow time for a party or a liturgy. You might want to look them over before your group decides on a closing celebration.)

- Close the meeting.

- "Coffee and."

## SUGGESTION FOR CLOSING

Continue with the Hope meditation. Start with the breathing exercises (see page 30). When the group has relaxed, read the following *slowly:*

Hope is Surprise at work.

A future awaits within each of us, yearning,
seeking life, fearful,
Catching up the past and the risk.

The love of another touches us, warms,
And in the slow pain of self-awareness each
chooses.

New energy bursts into the day.

A future awaits within us.

From the chaos of questions,
From the conflicts and responding trust,
From the sharing of life and the blend of dreams.

We reshape the past into a new beginning.

A future waiting in humanity.

A dream of an always more human people—
Struggling, planning, exchanging dreams.

*Concluding prayer:*

We pray to you now, Lord, for one very special
gift to ease our loneliness: the ability to understand and be understood, and, in this way, to
have our spirit touch others.

## DURING THE WEEK

*Reflection:* This asks the members to recall the loneliness
they felt during each stage of their lives—before they married, during their marriage, and now—and reflect on how
they coped with it. Writing a letter to a small loss is suggested as a way of recognizing how much we can miss
things and experiences as well as people, and of letting go
of one of these "small attachments."

*Self-Affirmation:* This exercise reinforces the reading by asking the members to recognize whatever successes, large or small, they have during each day. It emphasizes their strengths and talents in order to help them see themselves as complete people even though they are now single.

*Stress:* This offers two more image exercises. The first uses imagery to get rid of unpleasant thoughts. The second is a game of putting oneself in another person's shoes. Playing it will not only give the members some idea of how another person might view a situation, but also give them a chance to simulate saying exactly what they feel and think to that person.

**NOTES**

# session EIGHT

## Towards Growth

If your group has decided to hold additional closed sessions, reserve this session for the end of the program. If you have planned to continue, but as an open group, you may do this session either now or later.

*Introduction:* Seven weeks—even seven weeks of intensive work—is hardly enough time for divorced people to work through this "mourning period." Nevertheless, the time has come to set goals and begin planning for the future. This is the focus of this last session.

*Materials:* Same as for the preceding sessions, plus whatever supplies you need for your closing ceremony.

*Opening* (15–20 minutes): Open the meeting on time. Ask if anyone wishes to share something from his or her daily exercises. Ask if there is anything else any group members want to bring up. Make any necessary announcements.

*Reading* (5 minutes): Refer to page 97 in the participant's book. There will be only one reading and one exercise for this session. Ask for a volunteer to read aloud the first one or two paragraphs, and have other members continue the reading.

*Break into small groups,* if necessary. You will have to make your own determination as to the time limit for the discussion, given the special nature of this closing session.

*Exercise:* This asks the members to reflect on how they feel now about "letting go" of their marriage. By now, they should be combining some thinking with their feeling, and be able to start setting some goals for at least the immediate future.

*Five-Minute Warning:* Advise the members when they have five minutes to wind up their discussions.

*Closing:* If the members have been divided into sub-groups, bring them back together.

- Explain that our vocabulary plays a large part in establishing a new identity. Suggest that they read in the near future "Creating a New Vocabulary" on page 123 in the participant's book.

- Comment on the need for them to continue their daily exercises for self-affirmation and relaxation. Just because the program has ended doesn't mean that their need for this kind of real self-help has ended.

- Make some closing remarks of your own, thanking them in the name of the group for the support they have given each other during this program and for their patience, honesty, and concern.

- If they choose to keep meeting, but with a different format or a different group, advise them of other resources they can call upon and of any further assistance that you might be willing to offer.

- Ask whether anyone wants to add anything.
- Closing Ceremony. Choose one of the three suggestions on the following pages if your group did not develop a special closing.
- Have a celebration.

Relax. Congratulations! You did it!

---

## THREE OPTIONS FOR CLOSING THE FINAL SESSION

### SUGGESTION NO. ONE:

The following is a ceremony to symbolically let go of past hurts.

A) *MATERIALS:* A container covered with aluminum foil (suitable for burning papers), small blank papers, pencils, and matches or a lighter. *Note:* Be sure area where ceremony is to take place is well ventilated and fire safety precautions are taken.

B) Give two blank papers to each person.

C) Ask members to write on one slip of paper the *one* thing that they most want to let go of (e.g., guilt over one past thing, anger at a particular person, feeling badly over one thing).

D) Ask them to write on the second paper one promise to themselves (e.g., to do something positive for themselves every day; to forgive themselves or another; to work on one immediate, attainable goal; etc.).

E) When they have finished writing, collect the first paper and put in into the container.

F) Ask if any members wish to share with the group the promises they have made to themselves.

G) After each member who so desires has spoken, light the papers in the container and make some appropriate remarks in your own words. Here is an example:

> The papers in this container represent something you are willing to let go of, and in so doing, you are creating a change in yourself. From these ashes, like a phoenix, a new you is beginning to arise and grow. More time must pass before you are fully healed, but the exciting process of growth and change has begun, bringing with it the promise of a happy, fulfilled future. We have shared time and confidences with each other. We have worked and prayed together. Now, however, our time together is coming to an end. But what we've begun here will continue to grow because of your openness, willingness, and desire for a new life.
>
> Let's end our sessions, once again, on a note of hope.
>
> (Read the following meditation slowly:)
>
> Every beginning is a home for hope.
>
> Hope is the constant power and presence of God.
>
> Hope is our dynamic evolution into the future.
>
> Hope with a restlessness rooted in promise.
>
> Hope is the energy of the original dream that is always incomplete,

That always awaits our freedom.

We watch and wait.

We wait and hope, joyfully.

For the seeds to bring forth their fruit.

● ● ●

*SUGGESTION NO. TWO:*

On page 125, an essay by Bill Cane entitled "Celebrating the Steps Along the Way" continues our opening image of steps in journey. This reading expresses the spirit that we've tried to establish during these sessions—bad things did happen; people do care; pain can be a source of growth; and, with the help of God, divorced people can say, "We will not go back. We will keep going!"

You could ask the members to read this aloud (each one reading a paragraph or two) and end up by you reading the Hope meditation (see page 62 in this manual).

● ● ●

*SUGGESTION NO. THREE:*

On page 102 in the participant's book is a "Prayer for the Divorced" by Esther O. Fisher. Again, have the members take turns reading one stanza aloud, and conclude by you reading the last segment of the Hope meditation (see page 62 in this manual).

# NOTES

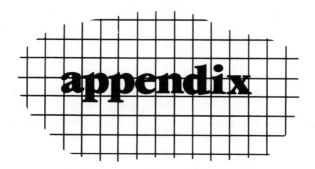

## OPTIONAL SESSIONS

The original commitment to this program was for eight sessions. However, some groups opt to continue meeting beyond this commitment. Two additional sessions are offered here should this need arise in your group.

*Forgiveness* and *Happiness* are both necessary for divorced people at this time, though many think they are unattainable. In both of these sessions, we've tried to emphasize just that . . . they can and should forgive; they can and should be happy. It is mentioned in the Participants' book that the members should read these essays and attempt the exercises on their own, if they decide not to use them as separate sessions.

## ADDED READINGS

*The Annulment Process,* by Rev. T. Tivy of Chicago Archdiocese, is an article stressing the healing aspect of the annulment process, rather than the legalese. It is a straight-forward approach to this complex, often misunderstood function of the Marriage Tribunal.

*Creating a New Vocabulary,* excerpted from N. Ricci's book, "Mom's House, Dad's House," stresses the importance of vocabulary on conduct, particularly when dealing with children.

*Celebrating the Steps Along the Way* is a chapter from Bill Cane's excellent book, "Through Crisis to Freedom." It continues on with the image of a journey we used to start this program, and stresses that even painful steps are still steps as long as they are forward-going. We suggested this as one of the alternate readings to closing the final session of the program.

We think all your group members will find all this material well worth the reading.

## BIBLIOGRAPHY

There are, of course, many excellent books on the market dealing with separation and divorce. The bibliography provided in the Participants' book includes just a sample of the best books written for divorced people. We have kept this section short, in hopes that the participants will be encouraged to continue on with their reading.

There is an expanded bibliography at the end of this Manual for those who are interested in seriously expanding their knowledge in this field.

**forgiveness**

**Introduction:** Divorced people will have a difficult time becoming free from the past until they begin to forgive both themselves and others. This, as the reading points out, is one of the hardest things of all for people to do. In fact, many divorced people don't even want to try, and so remain trapped in all the anger, guilt and bitterness of the past. This session attempts to begin the forgiveness process as a step towards new, freer beginnings.

**Materials:** Same as in previous sessions.

**Opening** (15–20 minutes): Open meeting on time. Make any necessary announcements. Inquire if anyone would like to share with the group anything that happened during the past week.

**Reading** (5 minutes): Refer to page 105 in the Participants' book. Ask for a volunteer to read the first two paragraphs. Proceed around the table, having the others read two paragraphs each.

**Break into sub-groups,** if necessary. Set the time when the discussions are to end, allowing time for the closing.

**Exercise One:** Focuses on identifying those people the members feel have hurt them; how they feel about forgiving these people; and how they might start learning to forgive.

**Exercise Two:** A "put yourself in another's shoes" exercise to see if the group members can help each other gain a different perspective.

**Five Minute Warning:** Advise the members when they have five minutes to wind up their discussions.

**Closing** (15–20 minutes): Bring the members together again, if they have been divided into sub-groups.

- Ask if anyone wishes to share anything with the other sub-groups.

- Since this is an optional session, we did not provide the participants with "During the Week" exercises. You might suggest here that those members who started keeping a notebook continue doing so this coming week. Recommend that they add to their story by writing down (in a more expanded form than they did in this session) how they think and feel about forgiving.

- Remind them also to keep up with the self-affirmation and anti-stress practices they've chosen in previous sessions.

- Close the meeting.

- "Coffee and."

## SUGGESTION FOR CLOSING

If you choose to keep up the theme of Hope, ask the members to turn to page 94 in the Participants' book and read silently, while you read aloud, Eugene Kennedy's insights into hope.

*Concluding prayer:*

> What better prayer could we say at this time, O Lord, than the words You, Yourself, gave us: "Forgive us our sins, as we forgive those who have sinned against us."

*Or*

If you wish, conclude with praying together the complete Lord's Prayer.

# NOTES

**Introduction:** Happiness means different things to different people, but, however one defines it, it is only achieved through a positive attitude toward life. Happiness grows out of peoples' interpretation of things that happen to them. This session endeavors to help divorced people change their perceptions and their habits, so as to make happiness a possibility for them.

**Materials:** Same as in previous sessions.

**Opening** (15–20 minutes): Open meeting on time. Make any necessary announcements. Inquire if anyone would like to share with the group anything that happened during the past week.

**Reading** (5 minutes): Refer to page 113 in the Participants' book. Ask for a volunteer to read the first two paragraphs. Proceed around the table, having the others read two paragraphs each.

*Break into sub-groups,* if necessary. Set the time when the discussions are to end, allowing time for the closing.

*Exercise One:* Ask members to write down what happiness means to them.

*Exercise Two:* Focuses on where members think happiness can be found for them, and what they can do to start developing the "habit of happiness." A practice exercise is offered.

*Five Minute Warning:* Advise the members when they have five minutes left to wind up their discussions.

*Closing* (15–20 minutes): Bring the members together again if they have been divided into sub-groups.

- Ask if anyone wishes to share anything with the other sub-groups.

- No "During the Week exercises are offered in the Participants' book. However, Question 4 in Exercise Two asked members to think of one or two things they could do to start developing the "happiness habit." You might urge the members to start practicing this habit this week as part of their self-affirmation efforts.

- Close the meeting.

- "Coffee and."


## SUGGESTION FOR CLOSING

The Beatitudes point the way to achieving Christian happiness. They would make an excellent meditation to close this session.

"How blest are the poor in spirit; the reign of
God is theirs.
Blest too are the sorrowing; they shall be con-
soled.
Blest are the lowly; they shall inherit the land.
Blest are they who hunger and thirst for holi-
ness; they shall have their fill.
Blest are they who show mercy;
mercy shall be theirs.
Blest are the single-hearted, for they shall see
God.
Blest too are the peacemakers; they shall be
called the sons of God.
Blest are those persecuted for holiness' sake;
the reign of God is theirs.
Blest are you when they insult you and perse-
cute you and utter every kind of slander
against you because of me.
Be glad and rejoice, for your reward is great in
heaven: they persecuted the prophets before
you in the very same way."

(Matthew 5:3–12)

### Concluding Prayer:

Remind us Lord
That with ordinary happiness you have over-
come all worlds of grief, and even now are
wrapping us in coats of common daily hap-
penings of goodness.
Strip us Lord
of melancholy strangeness, for we accept your
word—not that misery is unreal or painless—
but that all life is quick, shot through with
you, and therefore, fundamentally, with miles
and smiles of joy.

J. Carroll
(Tender of Wishes)

# bibliography

In the Participants' book, we listed some basic books and other sources of help to open more doors into dealing with divorce. For you facilitators who wish to push further into specific areas, or enrich your general knowledge about the divorce process, we recommend the following books:

## DIVORCE AND SEPARATION

Cassidy, R. *What Every Man Should Know about Divorce*. Washington, D.C.: New Republic Books, 1977.

An excellent book. The chapter on the emotional experience men undergo in the divorce process should be required reading for anyone dealing with divorce.

Grollman, E. and Sams, M. *Living Through Your Divorce*. Boston, Mass.: Beacon Press, 1978.

The book reads like a reassuring conversation with a wise personal counselor. Our only disappointment in reading is that we wanted more of it.

Hunt, M. & B. *The Divorce Experience*. New York, N.Y.: McGraw-Hill, 1977.

This book enables the reader to feel the intensity and immediacy of the divorce experiences from the painful process of separation and dissolution to gradual self-discovery and readjustment. Excellent research.

Kennedy, E. *Crisis Counseling*. New York, N.Y.: Continuum Books, 1981.

An essential guide for nonprofessional counselors who are running divorce groups. This book gives practical advice on related problems that may come up in the divorce groups.

Weiss, R. *Marital Separation.* New York, N.Y.: Basic Books, 1975.

This book will prove invaluable to the person involved in a separation, to the grown children of the separated and to those professionals who work with the newly separated or divorced.

Wrenn, L. *Divorce and Remarriage in the Catholic Church.* New York, N.Y.: Newman Press, 1973.

This book brings together ten persons holding different perspectives on the Catholic Tribunal system and its chief presupposition: that marriage is indissoluable.

Young, C.S.P., J., ed. *Ministering to the Divorced Catholic.* New York, N.Y.: Paulist Press, 1979.

An indispensable guidebook for those involved in the Divorced Catholics Ministry. This book deals realistically with the stereotypes and fears surrounding the complex problem of divorce. It makes use of sociological, theological and scriptural sources in constructing practical methods of ministry. Contributors include Charles E. Curran, Karl Lehmann, Bernard Haring, and Robert Weiss.

# PERSONAL GROWTH AND RELATIONSHIPS

Frankl, V. *Man's Search for Meaning.* New York, N.Y.: Random House, 1975.

Drawing on his 3-year experience in a concentration camp, Dr. Frankl's message is one of faith in a meaning of suffering. Each person, to survive, must weave the slender threads of his/her own life into a firm pattern of meaning and responsibility. "He who has a *why* to live can bear with almost any *how.*" Professional in content, written in laymen's language, this is a book well worth reading and re-reading.

Fromm, E. *The Art of Loving.* New York, N.Y.: Harper & Row, Inc., 1956.

A classic book explaining the process of loving in a profound way.

Kelsey, M. *Caring.* New York, N.Y.: Paulist Press, 1981.

Kelsey gives practical suggestions on how we can learn to love ourselves, listen to each other, understand our sexuality, face anger creatively and find greater intimacy in our relationships with our families and friends.

Krantzler, M. *Learning to Love Again.* New York, N.Y.: Thomas Y. Crowell Co., 1977.

An explanation of the many aspects of learning to love again after a divorce.

Powell, J. *Why Am I Afraid to Tell You Who I Am?* Niles, Ill.: Argus Communications, 1969.

A delightful book that will help people risk opening up and sharing themselves with others.

Ripple, P. *Walking with Loneliness.* Notre Dame, In.: Ave Maria Press, 1982.

A gentle book that helps divorced people look at loneliness, written with the sensitivity and experience born of Ms. Ripple's many years experience in her ministry to the divorced and separated.

Rubin, T. *The Angry Book.* New York, N.Y.: Avon, 1969.

Another excellent book for understanding and dealing with anger.

Peck, M. *The Road Less Traveled*. New York, N.Y.: Simon & Schuster, 1978.

A highly readable book that is valuable and sometimes brilliant in its insistence that there is no distinction between achieving spiritual growth and achieving mental growth. The comments on love are marked by freshness and originality.

Ulene, A. *Feeling Fine*. Los Angeles, Ca.: J. T. Tarcher, Inc., 1977.

A twenty-day program that contains hundreds of pleasurable activities to fit into your lifestyle. This is the type of book you buy to treat yourself.

Weiss, R. *Loneliness*. Cambridge, Mass.: The MIT Press, 1973.

Another excellent study of loneliness that offers many compelling insights.

## CHILDREN OF DIVORCE

Galper, M. *Co-Parenting*. Philadelphis, Pa.: Running Press, 1978.

The author describes an alternative to the more traditional forms of custody arrangements. A good book for professionals.

Gardner, R. *The Boys and Girls Book About Divorce*. New York, N.Y.: Science House, Inc., 1970.

Written at the junior high school reading level, this is a book many kids can read by themselves. Better still, they can read it with their parents.

Gardner, R. *The Parents Book about Divorce*. New York, N.Y.: Doubleday, 1977.

Dr. Gardner continues his work with children of divorced parents with this book directed towards the parents.

Ricci, I. *Mom's House, Dad's House*. New York, N.Y.: MacMillan Publishing Co., 1980.

A resource book for parents, professionals and educators. It describes the divorce process in detail and the two-home approach to child rearing.

Visher, E. & J. *Step-Families*. Secaucus, N.J.: The Citadel Press, 1980.

An analysis of the problems of the individual adult, the couple, and the children in the remarried families. It offers a host of therapeutic and preventive techniques. A book of caring and dedication.